THE GREAT

written by
Rachel Gregory

illustrations by
Jack Foster

Contact The Author:
Email: info@rachelgreg.com
Website: rachelgreg.com
Instagram: Rachelgreg_

Copyright © 2019 Rachel Gregory
Illustrated by Jack Foster
All rights reserved.

No part of this book may be reproduced in any manner without the written consent of the publisher except for brief excerpts in critical reviews or articles.

ISBN: 978-1-61244-729-2
Library of Congress Control Number: 2019903999

Printed in the United States of America

Halo Publishing International
1100 NW Loop 410
Suite 700 - 176
San Antonio, Texas 78213
www.halopublishing.com
contact@halopublishing.com

To our son, Konnor Maxwell Smith.
We will always love you.

Summer was over, and it was the first day back to school. Gracie could hardly sit still on the ride to school. "I'm so excited to be in the third grade!" She excitingly said.

Her father chuckled. "Well, don't bounce yourself out of the car. I would like to get you there safely."

When they arrived at Orchid Elementary School, Gracie jumped out of the car. She blew a kiss to her parents and ran to see her friends.

The kids all chattered about the fun they had during summer break.

"What did you do?" Gracie's friend, Sally, asked her.

Gracie shrugged. "Well. . ."

But before Gracie could say any more, the bell rang, and all the children lined up and shuffled into school.

Gracie walked into her new third-grade classroom. Her teacher, Mrs. Center, was standing behind her desk.

"Welcome to third grade," Mrs. Center said. "Please look for your names on the desks, and take a seat. After I take attendance, we'll start the day by sharing what we did over the summer. If you have any questions, just remember to raise your hand and be polite."

After checking off everyone's name in the attendance book, Mrs. Center asked, "Who would like to go first?"

The kids squirmed in their seats. No one wanted to go first. Gracie looked around and slowly raised her hand. "I'll go first, Mrs. Center."

Although she was shy, Gracie wanted to be brave. She got up and began telling her story. "Today I am going to tell you about my great baby brother." She hesitated.

"You can do it, Gracie," Mrs. Center reassured her.

"On June second, my mom had a baby boy," Gracie said. "We named him Max Henry, but he was born too early. The doctor said that's called premature, but I can say preemie. His hands and feet were super small. He was small all over!" Her voice started getting stronger.

"The doctor said he needed to be put in an incubator," Gracie added.

Robert raised his hand. "What's an incubator?"

"It is a place where preemie babies go to get strong," Gracie answered him.

She held up a picture. "Here he is in the incubator. He spent three days there, but we saw him every day. He would move his tiny hands and feet when Mom would read or sing to him. The nurses said he was a great fighter, so we all called him The Great!"

"Did the doctors call him The Great too?" Timothy raised his hand and asked.

"Yes, they did. They'd stop by, lean over the incubator, and ask, 'How's Baby Great doing today?' It sounded so funny when a big doctor talked in a little voice. It made me laugh every time," Gracie said.

She giggled and the class laughed with her.

Gracie went on, "Although my brother was a great fighter, he went to heaven a few days later. I cried, but Mom hugged me and said that it was okay, Grandma will look after him in heaven."

Although it had been a few months, Gracie still felt sad at times. Standing in front of the class, she blinked her eyes and sniffed.

Mrs. Center came to stand next to her. "It's okay to be sad."

"I know," Gracie responded softly. Then, she took a big breath and continued her story.

"After Max went to heaven, we gave him a going away party. Some of my mom's friends called it a funeral. Lots of friends and family came. And there were flowers, too."

Emma raised her hand and asked, "What did you wear, Gracie?"

"I wore a white dress. So did Mom." Gracie grinned. "Max wore a white outfit, too. Even his little airplane was white."

Timothy excitedly raised his hands and asked, "Was it a real airplane?"

Gracie shook her head. "No, it was a small, special airplane for Max to lie in. Here's a picture."

The kids all leaned forward to see.

Gracie continued, "On our way home after saying goodbye to Max, I asked Mom and Dad if Max was up there with the stars. Dad said he had a good idea; he would help me to make a Forever Star for Max when we got home. This way he is forever in my heart."

Sally raised her hand. "How do you make a Forever Star?" she asked.

"It's like arts and crafts. With your parent's help, you cut out a star and put the name of your family member who has gone to heaven on it with a nice note," Gracie answered. "My note for my baby brother reads- 'Let's Travel The World Forever - The Great.'"

"Can we make Forever Stars, Mrs. Center?" Gracie asked.

"That's a great idea," Mrs. Center replied. "I'll send home a note explaining what we would like to do. If your parents agree, we'll do just that."

This idea made Gracie very happy.

The kids were all excited about the story. They looked forward to making their own stars and naming them.

"I will make a star for my grandpa," Susan added.

"I will make one for My Dad, too; he's my superhero," Harry said.

Aaron nodded. "I'll make one for my mom, who I miss so much, but Dad said she'll always be in my heart."

Rick clapped his hands. "I'll make one for my dog, Fluffy."

Mrs. Center said, "I will also be making a beautiful star for my mother." She turned to Gracie. "Well done! You are such a brave girl for sharing your story."

Gracie felt happy that her class would be making Forever Stars for their family members and pets that had gone to heaven. And now the entire class knows that it is OK to be sad, but their loved ones are not alone.

Gracie hoped that Max would be proud of her, as The Great big sister.

The End

You can also make your own star at home as a family project!

Step 1
Choose a piece of letter-size paper in your loved one's favorite color. Fold the paper in half. Ensure that the paper is positioned upright at all times. See the arrow below.

Step 2
Fold the paper in half a second time. Then, unfold the paper. You will use the crease (Point A) as the guiding line for the next step.

Step 3
Using the crease as a guideline, fold the bottom right corner up towards the crease (Point A).

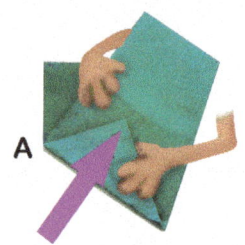

Step 4
Now, fold the bottom left corner over the right edge.

Step 5
Fold the top right corner over the left edge.

Step 6
With the help of a parent, use scissors to cut a diagonal line for your star.

Step 7
Now unfold to reveal your very own Forever Star.

Step 8
Use a hole puncher to make a hole in the top of the star. Pull a small piece of string through the hole so that you can hang it in your home. You may also choose to laminate the star so that it will last longer.

Born in Grand Turk, Turks & Caicos, Rachel Gregoire has lived in both Massachusetts and Florida where she completed her undergraduate degree. Returning to the Turks & Caicos, she continued her studies online at the University of Liverpool. She completed her master's degree in International Finance and Accounting, and shortly after, she was accepted to the University of Walden to pursue her doctorate in Business Administration.

Rachel is the mother of a beautiful daughter. In addition to her background in finance, she is an author and a hotelier. She truly believes that no one should allow their pain and adversity to defeat them but instead turn it into something beautiful. She has a genuine passion for others; she enjoys writing, reading, playing the violin, running, and traveling.

After losing her dear son to extreme prematurity, Rachel became a founding member of the Turks & Caicos Premature Foundation: finding purpose in every loss.

Jack Foster has illustrated over 70 children's books. He lives outside of Chicago with his lovely wife, Aleithia, and their cat, Jasper. He has five grown children and fourteen terrific grandchildren who keep him young. Foster attended the American Academy of Art in Chicago. You can check out his work and his books at jackfosterart.com.

Lightning Source UK Ltd.
Milton Keynes UK
UKHW050425271119
354259UK00005B/23/P